LEONARD INSTRUMENTAL PLAY ALONG

CLASSICAL SOLOS FOR TRUMPET

VOLUME 2

TITLE	PAGE	FULL PERFORMANCE TRACK	ACCOMPANIMENT ONLY TRACK
Largo (from *Xerxes*)	2	1	16
Songs My Mother Taught Me (from *Gypsy Songs*)	3	2	
Minuet No. 2 (from *Notebook from Anna Magdalena Bach*)	4	3	
La Cinquantaine (from *Two Pieces for Cello and Piano*)	5	4	
See, the Conquering Hero Comes (from *Judas Maccabeus*)	6	5	20
Sonatina (Op. 36, No. 1)	7	6	21
Serenata (from *String Quartet, Op. 3, No. 5*)	8	7	22
Tambourin (from *Second Suite in E Minor*)	9	8	23
Waltz (from *Album for the Young*)	10	9	24
Sonatina (from *Six Pieces, Op. 3*)	11	10	25
Gavotte (from *Paride ed Elena*)	12	11	26
Sonata (Op. 118, No. 1)	13	12	27
Serenade (from *Schwanengesang, D. 957*)	14	13	28
Sonatina (Anh. 5, No. 1)	15	14	29
Bourrée (from *Flute Sonata, HWV 363b*)	16	15	30
B♭ Tuning Notes			31

The enclosed audio CD is also a CD-ROM and includes:
Piano accompaniment for each solo in PDF format for printing.
Tempo Adjustment Software for use with most PC or Mac computers. Instructions included.

ISBN 978-1-4803-5121-9

HAL•LEONARD® CORPORATION

7777 W. BLUEMOUND RD. P.O. BOX 13819 MILWAUKEE, WI 53213

Visit Hal Leonard Online at
www.halleonard.com

LARGO
from *Xerxes*

GEORGE FRIDERIC HANDEL
Arranged by PHILIP SPARKE

B♭ TRUMPET

Largo (♩ = 68)

00121143

SONGS MY MOTHER TAUGHT ME

from *Gypsy Songs*

ANTONÍN DVOŘÁK
Arranged by PHILIP SPARKE

B♭ TRUMPET

Andante con moto
(♩ = 108)

MINUET NO. 2
from *Notebook for Anna Magdalena Bach*

Bb TRUMPET

Attributed to CHRISTIAN PEZOLD
Arranged by PHILIP SPARKE

00121143

LA CINQUANTAINE

from *Two Pieces for Cello and Piano*

JEAN GABRIEL-MARIE
Arranged by PHILIP SPARKE

B♭ TRUMPET

SEE, THE CONQUERING HERO COMES

from *Judas Maccabeus*

B♭ TRUMPET

GEORGE FRIDERIC HANDEL
Arranged by PHILIP SPARKE

Allegro (♩ = 132)

00121143

SONATINA
Op. 36, No. 1

MUZIO CLEMENTI
Arranged by PHILIP SPARKE

B♭ TRUMPET

Allegro (♩ = 88)

SERENATA
from *String Quartet, Op. 3, No. 5*

FRANZ JOSEPH HAYDN
Arranged by PHILIP SPARKE

B♭ TRUMPET

TAMBOURIN
from *Second Suite in E Minor*

JEAN-PHILIPPE RAMEAU
Arranged by PHILIP SPARKE

B♭ TRUMPET

WALTZ
from *Album for the Young*

PYOTR ILYICH TCHAIKOVSKY
Arranged by PHILIP SPARKE

Bb TRUMPET

SONATINA
from *Six Pieces, Op. 3*

CARL MARIA VON WEBER
Arranged by PHILIP SPARKE

B♭ TRUMPET

GAVOTTE
from *Paride ed Elena*

CHRISTOPH GLUCK/arr. JOHANNES BRAHMS
Arranged by PHILIP SPARKE

B♭ TRUMPET

00121143

SONATA
Op. 118, No. 1

ROBERT SCHUMANN
Arranged by PHILIP SPARKE

B♭ TRUMPET

00121143

SERENADE
from *Schwanengesang, D.957*

FRANZ SCHUBERT
Arranged by PHILIP SPARKE

B♭ TRUMPET

Andante con moto
(♩ = 84)

00121143

SONATINA
Anh. 5, No. 1

LUDWIG VAN BEETHOVEN
Arranged by PHILIP SPARKE

B♭ TRUMPET

Moderato (♩ = 126)

00121143

BOURRÉE

from *Flute Sonata, HWV 363b*

B♭ TRUMPET

GEORGE FRIDERIC HANDEL
Arranged by PHILIP SPARKE

00121143